mic drop moments
journal

TO:

....

FROM:

....

mic drop moments

journal

Inspirational One-Liners

W PUBLISHING GROUP

AN IMPRINT OF THOMAS NELSON

Mic Drop Moments Journal

© 2023 W Publishing

Published in Nashville, Tennessee, by W Publishing, an imprint of Thomas Nelson.

Thomas Nelson titles may be purchased in bulk for educational, business, fundraising, or sales promotional use. For information, please e-mail SpecialMarkets@ThomasNelson.com.

Any internet addresses, phone numbers, or company or product information printed in this book are offered as a resource and are not intended in any way to be or to imply an endorsement by Thomas Nelson, nor does Thomas Nelson vouch for the existence, content, or services of these sites, phone numbers, companies, or products beyond the life of this book.

ISBN 978-0-7852-9330-9 (TP)

Interior design: Emily Ghattas

Printed in the United States of America

23 24 25 26 LSC 6 5 4 3 2 1

Contents

Introduction

....

Did you know that journaling creates awareness, regulates emotions, promotes a growth mindset, encourages openness, and provides inspiration? Writing down your thoughts and feelings on a regular basis can be a healthy coping strategy by increasing mindfulness of emotions and building insight.

When things get tough, people often turn to motivational quotes to provide inspiration, healing, or hope. A single quote lets you know that you're not alone. Someone has felt the same feelings. Someone has gone through a similar season. Someone overcame. There's a sense of unspoken solidarity in a quote.

In *Mic Drop Moments Journal* you'll read inspirational quotes and have space to write down your reflections. You don't have to work through the journal from front to back—start and stop wherever you'd like. Make journaling a habit by carving out ten to fifteen minutes a day to reflect. It's a ritual that's worth your time!

Part 1

Moments with Jennie Allen

We have become a generation *obsessed* with understanding *ourselves,* as if that holds the *answer* for our restless, discontent souls.

—*RESTLESS*

Reflect

....

What are you obsessed with understanding about yourself? How can you let go of this obsession and shift your focus to contentment? How will the newfound contentment change your being?

....

....

....

....

....

....

....

....

....

....

....

Do your *everyday* and your *ordinary*. Godliness is *found* and *formed* in those places.

—*MADE FOR THIS*

Reflect

....

Where have you seen God recently? It could be as simple as a rainbow after a storm or hearing the perfect song after a long day.

....

....

....

....

....

....

....

....

....

....

....

....

I think God can *untangle* your soul, your story, your gifts, your people, your place, *and* your passions, and He can begin to *weave* them all into purposes that you haven't been brave *enough* to imagine.

—MADE FOR THIS

Reflect

....

Close your eyes and take a deep breath. Don't overthink these questions but answer honestly. What do you do well? What do your friends say you do well? If you could do or be anything, what would you do or be?

....

....

....

....

....

....

....

....

....

....

....

I know it feels near ridiculous to *live* for things we can't yet see. At the base of our *souls*, each of us needs to figure out whether we are *building* God's glory or our own.

—*MADE FOR THIS*

Reflect

....

What does it mean, to you, to be created for God's glory?

....
....
....
....
....
....
....
....
....
....
....
....
....

Out of our pain we *heal.*
Out of our bondage we
set *free.* And, again,
the *messiest* waste of
our lives becomes
the *most* fertile soil.

—*MADE FOR THIS*

Reflect

....

Our pain pushes us to grow and love ourselves. It is during painful times when we realize our strengths and resilience. Think back on a difficult time or season. What did you learn and how did you become stronger? How did that time change your future?

....
....
....
....
....
....
....
....
....
....
....

Part 2

Moments with
Andy Andrews

Most people *think* it takes a long time to *change*. It doesn't. Change is immediate! *Instantaneous*! It may take a long time to *decide* to change . . . but change happens in a *heartbeat*!

—*THE NOTICER*

Reflect

....

When did deciding to change take a long time for you?
How did that decision impact your future?

....
....
....
....
....
....
....
....
....
....
....
....
....
....

Success *requires* the emotional balance of a *committed* heart. When confronted with a challenge, the *committed* heart will search for a solution. The undecided heart *searches* for an escape.

—*THE TRAVELER'S GIFT*

Reflect

....

Is there a solution you need help creating? What can you do to shift your commitment toward finding a solution?

....

....

....

....

....

....

....

....

....

....

....

....

One way to define *wisdom* is the ability to see, into the *future*, the consequences of your choices in the *present*. That ability can give you a *completely* different perspective on what the *future* might look like.

—*THE NOTICER*

Reflect

....

Write down three things that you would like to look different in your future. Once your list is created, think about the things you need to do to make those three things happen. Now write down what changes you need to make so you can achieve this future you're envisioning.

....

....

....

....

....

....

....

....

....

....

Life itself is a privilege, but to live life to the fullest—well, that is a choice.

—*THE TRAVELER'S GIFT*

Reflect

....

What are some ways you can live your life in a fuller way?

....

....

....

....

....

....

....

....

....

....

....

....

....

In *desperate* times, much more than anything else, folks need *perspective*. For perspective brings calm. *Calm* leads to clear thinking. Clear thinking yields *new* ideas. And ideas produce the *bloom* . . . of an answer. Keep your head and heart clear. *Perspective* can just as easily be lost as it can be found.

—*THE NOTICER*

Reflect

....

Jot down some of the new ideas you've produced. If you've lost perspective, take time to shift your perspective and calm down. Then revisit this page and jot down the ideas that bloomed.

....

....

....

....

....

....

....

....

....

....

....

Part 3

Moments with
Kat Armstrong

Hope, real hope, is certainty that a *loving* God will come from outside our *circumstances*, enter into our messy reality, and be with us *through* it all as he works everything out for our good.

—*THE IN-BETWEEN PLACE*

Reflect

....

Can you think of a time you felt hopeless? How did God reveal Himself and come alongside your messy reality to restore your hope?

....

....

....

....

....

....

....

....

....

....

....

....

Your rock and a hard place *might* be a transition at work . . .

—*THE IN-BETWEEN PLACE*

Reflect

....

When was the last time you hit rock bottom? How did you evolve into a stronger individual after going through that challenging time? Did that difficult season help you process things differently for the future?

....

....

....

....

....

....

....

....

....

....

....

By connecting *love* for God with love for *ourselves* and others, it's clear Jesus is teaching us that *surrender* and *obedience* are connected to our flourishing and are *blessings* to everyone around us.

—*NO MORE HOLDING BACK*

Reflect

....

Write down three ways your surrender and obedience have blessed others. Now write down three more ways you can bless others with your surrender and obedience.

....

....

....

....

....

....

....

....

....

....

....

....

We may not *have* a lot to offer, but we must learn the *sacred* practice of offering everything.

—*NO MORE HOLDING BACK*

Reflect

....

An offering should never be judged by its quantity but rather by its quality. Reflect on a gift or gesture you've received that was small in size but impacted you greatly. What was that gift or gesture? Who gave it to you? How did it impact your life?

....

....

....

....

....

....

....

....

....

....

Part 9

Moments with Valorie Burton

The fact that *living* with no breathing room has *become* the norm for a large segment of the population is a threat to our *well-being* and *happiness*. There is an undeniable connection between *time* and *happiness*.

—*IT'S ABOUT TIME*

Reflect

....

Are you consistently emotionally and physically tired? If you replied yes, how can you make time for happiness? Make a list of tasks and obligations that don't bring you joy. What can you let go of? What can you delegate to someone else? What can you stop doing? It's okay to say no and nothing more. Your happiness is more important than checking something off a to-do list.

....

....

....

....

....

....

....

....

....

....

I want for you what I wanted for *myself*—to stop feeling guilty about things you *haven't* done wrong.

—*LET GO OF THE GUILT*

Reflect

·······················

Have you apologized for things out of your control or things you didn't do? Guilt can take on many forms—natural guilt, free-floating or toxic guilt, and existential guilt. It is important to have affirmations in place to prohibit guilt from creating self-sabotaging behavior and negative thoughts.

Write down three to five affirmations you can use next time you're feeling guilty for things you haven't done wrong. Here are a few affirmations to get you started:

- I am worthy of happiness and peace.
- I am abundant in light and love.
- I release the stories that make me feel small.
- I allow myself to move forward in life.

···

···

···

···

···

When we take for granted the *gift* of time, we spend it as though our lives are a dress *rehearsal* and we'll get to come back later for the *real* performance.

—*IT'S ABOUT TIME*

Reflect

....

Make a list of the things you should be making time
for. Beside each thing, list something you can give up in
order to create time for what matters.

....

....

....

....

....

....

....

....

....

....

....

....

....

Just as there are timeless *choices*, there are also false urgencies.

—*IT'S ABOUT TIME*

Reflect

....

False urgencies are situations we flag urgent, but later will mean little or nothing in the future. You may not even remember why they were important or who they involved. We are intentionally bombarded with messages that wear away the boundary between real and created urgency. How can you re-establish your boundaries? What recent false urgencies did you believe were urgent?

....

....

....

....

....

....

....

....

....

....

Part 5

Moments with
Lara Casey

I'm learning that there is *magic* in the middle ground.

—*CULTIVATE*

Reflect

....

The middle ground is the compromise. It is the agreement between two extreme positions, options, or objectives. Oftentimes the middle ground reflects our growth as individuals, as a couple, as friends, as family members, and as neighbors. What magic can you find in your middle ground?

....

....

....

....

....

....

....

....

....

Embracing the imperfect

is *essential* to growing

what matters.

—*CULTIVATE*

Reflect

....

How has imperfection aided in your growth as a human being? How do you embrace your imperfections on a regular basis? What can you do to actively embrace the imperfections of others?

....

....

....

....

....

....

....

....

....

....

....

Slow growth is

still growth.

—*CULTIVATE*

Reflect

....

Real growth takes time, and it is different for everyone. Oftentimes humans struggle with the patience and intentionality that growth requires. Can you think of a time you tried to rush growth? What was the outcome? Can you think of a time growth felt slow? What was the outcome?

....

....

....

....

....

....

....

....

....

....

No matter what mistakes
you've *made* or will make,
you don't have to rely
on your own *strength*
to grow this life.

—*CULTIVATE*

Reflect

....

Everyone makes mistakes. What mistake have you made that required other people to help you learn a lesson and grow? How has that mistake changed your life?

....

....

....

....

....

....

....

....

....

....

....

....

Sometimes God uses another person to *plant* a seed in our lives. And sometimes that seed doesn't *sprout* till decades later—right on time.

—*CULTIVATE*

Reflect

....

Which people in your life have planted seeds that shifted your path and changed your life? How would your life be different without these people and/or without the seeds they've planted?

....

....

....

....

....

....

....

....

....

....

....

Cultivating what matters
is worth every bit of what
we *give up* in time, pride,
money, possessions,
status, or comfort.

—*CULTIVATE*

Reflect

....

What matters most to you? Make a list. What have you given up to cultivate what matters?

....

....

....

....

....

....

....

....

....

....

....

....

....

Part 6

Moments with
Jess Ekstrom

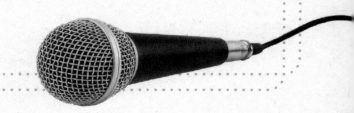

Why optimism? Because *anyone* who has ever done something great had to *believe* in something better than the present.

—*CHASING THE BRIGHT SIDE*

Reflect

....

Think about a situation that felt less than great. How did your optimism become a game changer? If you weren't optimistic, how could a positive mindset have changed the outcome?

....

....

....

....

....

....

....

....

....

....

....

....

Everything we want is *within* our grasp if we're willing to throw *perfection* out the door and embrace the messiness of the *journey*.

—*CHASING THE BRIGHT SIDE*

Reflect

....

Perfectionism is stressful and perfection is unattainable. What are some ways you can embrace the mess and throw out perfection?

....

....

....

....

....

....

....

....

....

....

....

....

....

We can't *control* our experiences, but we can always *write* our stories.

—*CHASING THE BRIGHT SIDE*

Reflect

....

Think of a recent experience when you had no control whatsoever. How did that make you feel? How did the experience shift your perspective and opinions? How did you respond to write your own story?

....

....

....

....

....

....

....

....

....

....

....

....

Let the *wonder* be

bigger than the limits.

—*CHASING THE BRIGHT SIDE*

Reflect

....

How are you affecting your success by placing limits on your ability to wonder and dream? What are some ways you can have a growth mindset and become more open to wonder?

....
....
....
....
....
....
....
....
....
....
....
....

Part 7

Moments with
Laurieann Gibson

Staying in touch with our dreams *matters* more than most of us ever talk about.

—*DANCE YOUR DANCE*

Reflect

....

What are some dreams that you've given up on? What steps can you take to revitalize those dreams and make them into a reality?

....
....
....
....
....
....
....
....
....
....
....
....

Sometimes it feels like everyone's *trying* to be someone else, someone other *than* who they are from the inside out, because *people* tell them that that's what they need to do or are *supposed* to do in order to be successful.

—*DANCE YOUR DANCE*

Reflect

....

Reflect on a time when you were expected to do something because it would make you successful. Did you listen to society? If not, how did your decision to go against the norm redefine the meaning of success for you?

....
....
....
....
....
....
....
....
....
....
....

The *passion* inside you is a gift from God, which can *express* itself in all sorts of ways and can give you a level of success and *completeness* that's greater than anything society's rules and games and false measures of *success* can ever offer.

—*DANCE YOUR DANCE*

Reflect

....

What is the passion that God gifted you? How has that passion impacted who you are as an individual?

....

....

....

....

....

....

....

....

....

....

....

....

....

We all learn lessons
as we *make* our way
through life, and whatever
you're doing right now is
definitely *teaching* you
something you need.

—*DANCE YOUR DANCE*

Reflect

....

Life is all about learning. What are some of the most valuable lessons you've learned? How have those lessons shaped your present and future?

....

....

....

....

....

....

....

....

....

....

....

....

Part 8

Moments with
Scott Hamilton

Winning is about accessing all of your innate human potential. You *cannot* be born a winner. But you can become.

—*FINISH FIRST*

Reflect

....

How have you become a winner? What experiences, people, and hard truths made you into a winner?

....
....
....
....
....
....
....
....
....
....
....
....
....

If there were a recipe for

winning, losing would

be a main ingredient.

—*FINISH FIRST*

Reflect

....

Losing makes us better. It teaches us vulnerability, how to improve, humility, patience, sacrifice, and gratitude. Think about a time when losing made you a better human being. What did you gain from your loss? How did your loss motivate you? What was the lesson you learned from losing?

....

....

....

....

....

....

....

....

....

....

My faith tells me that everything is *meaningful,* that nothing happens by accident. *You* are here for a reason. If you don't know that reason yet, *you* are probably struggling and miserable.

—*FINISH FIRST*

Reflect

. . . .

Be honest: Do you know your reason? If you do, say it out loud. Then write down why your reason makes you incredible. If you don't know your reason, make a list of the things that you're good at. Reference this list every day and read each thing out loud. Keep reciting and adding to your list until you truly believe and understand your reason.

. . . .

. . . .

. . . .

. . . .

. . . .

. . . .

. . . .

. . . .

. . . .

. . . .

Purpose is the difference between a pipe dream and a goal *worth* all the sacrifice it will take to get it. *Purpose* is the difference between your ego telling you to do something and *God* telling you to do it.

—*FINISH FIRST*

Reflect

....

Do you know the difference between a pipe dream and purpose? Make two columns. In one write *pipe dream* and in the other write *purpose*. Create a list for both entities. Can you recognize how your value is ingrained in your purpose? This doesn't mean you can't have pipe dreams, because sometimes pipe dreams morph into purpose. How has God led you to identify your purpose?

....

....

....

....

....

....

....

....

....

....

Part 9

Moments with
Levi Lusko

You can't win a

conflict that you don't

admit you are in.

—*DECLARE WAR*

Reflect

....

The first step in conflict resolution is to admit that there is a problem. Think about a time when you mishandled a conflict. How should you have resolved the problem? What did you learn from the situation? What steps can you take to be a better conflict solver?

....
....
....
....
....
....
....
....
....
....
....

If you take a *selfie*, you won't see the version of *yourself* you are meant to become, no matter what *filter* you use.

—*THROUGH THE EYES OF A LION*

Reflect

....

Be honest: What is the purpose of a filter? Your friends and family already know what you really look like. Applying a filter creates an untrue version of you that doesn't really exist. We all have flaws, but we should look for ways to embrace them. Create a list of ways you can build your self-confidence and self-esteem. Then do the work so you can begin to appreciate the unfiltered you.

....

....

....

....

....

....

....

....

....

....

The fingerprints of God
are often *invisible* until
you look at them in
the rearview mirror.

—*THROUGH THE EYES OF A LION*

Reflect

....

Have you ever prayed to God and been left with unanswered prayers? Oftentimes those unanswered prayers are fingerprints from God and a part of His plan. Can you think of a time when you realized that God was at work the whole time without you ever knowing?

....

....

....

....

....

....

....

....

....

....

Hard times are a *passport* that gives you permission *to go places* you wouldn't get to any other way.

—THROUGH THE EYES OF A LION

Reflect

....

Think about a difficult time you've experienced or a dark season you've endured. How did those hard times make you stronger? How did you grow from that experience? Did anything bloom from your hard times?

....

....

....

....

....

....

....

....

....

....

....

....

Because of Jesus, we have *hope*. And because of hope, even in the midst of the worst *storms* of this life, we have an *anchor* for our souls.

—*THROUGH THE EYES OF A LION*

Reflect

....

Hope is an optimistic state of mind that is based on an expectation of positive outcomes. What can you do to keep your hope alive and thriving?

....
....
....
....
....
....
....
....
....
....
....
....
....

Part 10

Moments with
Robert Morgan

When you find yourself *between* sword and sea, remember that difficult times can sensitize us to *God's* nearness.

—*THE RED SEA RULES*

Reflect

....

Think of a time you didn't think God was nearby. What occurred to make your view or opinion change? What can you do in the future to remind yourself that God is always with you?

....

....

....

....

....

....

....

....

....

....

....

The Lord *delights* in

the impossible.

—THE RED SEA RULES

Reflect

....

What are some examples of the Lord showing up for you in impossible ways?

....

....

....

....

....

....

....

....

....

....

....

....

....

You can bury worry

before worry buries you.

—*WORRY LESS, LIVE MORE*

Reflect

....

Everyone worries, but we must have faith that everything will work out. What are some simple ways you can put your worries in check and hand them to the Lord?

....
....
....
....
....
....
....
....
....
....
....
....
....

Take things *moment by moment,* and when you don't know what to do, just do what comes next. Trust God to *lead* you a step at a time.

—*THE RED SEA RULES*

Reflect

....

When events are stressful, it's not uncommon to feel overwhelmed and worried. The best way to approach a solution is to take it step-by-step. Write down affirmations that will keep you grounded and focused during these times.

....

....

....

....

....

....

....

....

....

....

....

Part 11

Moments with Mattie Jackson Selecman

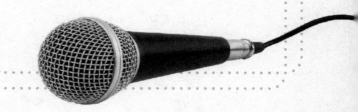

Grief is not a one-way street *toward* healing. We can't climb a ladder or check off boxes to reach a better day. *Everyone's* grief, and every day of grief, looks different.

—*LEMONS ON FRIDAY*

Reflect

....

What surprised you the most about grief you recently experienced? How has grief changed your life? How has grief made you more compassionate and vulnerable?

....

....

....

....

....

....

....

....

....

....

....

....

....

When life gives us *lemons,* only a long, grueling process can turn them into *lemonade.* It hurts every step of the way because the process is *dependent* on God's plan and God's timing, which almost always play out differently *than* we'd like.

—*LEMONS ON FRIDAY*

Reflect

....

Think about a time when God's plan and timing didn't sync up with yours. In the moment, it felt impossible to see positivity or embrace a new plan. Looking back, can you reflect on what you've learned and how you've grown because of the experience?

....

....

....

....

....

....

....

....

....

....

....

Our God knows the

deepest caverns

of sorrow.

—*LEMONS ON FRIDAY*

Reflect

....

When you're in the thick of sadness, it might feel like God doesn't understand. But He does! He made the ultimate sacrifice. Write down any sorrow that you're experiencing and pray to God. Allow Him to come alongside you and provide comfort.

....
....
....
....
....
....
....
....
....
....
....

My healing was now in the hands of *the One* who makes mountains out of mustard seeds, wine out of water, *and* beauty out of ashes.

—*LEMONS ON FRIDAY*

Reflect

....

Once we realize that He's in control, we can create hope and wonder. How can you nurture your healing journey with your faith in God? How can you deepen your relationship with the One?

....

....

....

....

....

....

....

....

....

....

....

If you were inspired by their mic drop moments, check out the books featuring these inspirational one-liners.

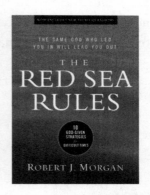

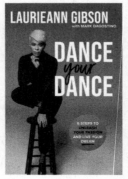

LEMONS ON FRIDAY

TRUSTING GOD THROUGH MY GREATEST HEARTBREAK

MATTIE JACKSON SELECMAN

FOREWORD BY JAMIE IVEY

KAT ARMSTRONG

THE IN-BETWEEN PLACE

WHERE JESUS CHANGES YOUR STORY

Kat Armstrong

NO MORE HOLDING BACK

Emboldening Women to Move Past Barriers, See Their Worth, and Serve God Everywhere

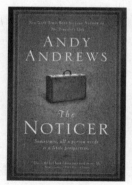

ANDY ANDREWS

The NOTICER

Sometimes, all a person needs is a little perspective.

ROBERT J. MORGAN

Author of Red Sea Rules and The Strength You Need

WORRY LESS LIVE MORE

God's Prescription for a Better Life

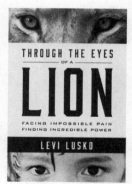

THROUGH THE EYES OF A LION

FACING IMPOSSIBLE PAIN FINDING INCREDIBLE POWER

LEVI LUSKO

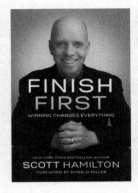

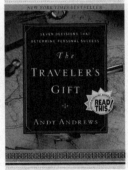